Praise for *"Doggy's Minnesota Winter"*

"Doggy's Minnesota Winter" is the best book by Ms. Flaagan yet! Her lovable dog is joined by her adorable "people friends" while they tell the story that so many people around the world just don't understand… the LOVE of Minnesota winters! I love how Ella shows us the fun adventures people and their dogs take together in the wintertime. As she does in all of her books, each page keeps young readers entertained and involved through the use of the prediction questions. This helps them to easily relate to the characters and activities. I am giving *Doggy's Minnesota Winter* to my childrens' classrooms because it is the perfect book for making early reading skills FUN to learn. It's obvious that the author is a teacher! This book will be enjoyed for many, many years to come.

~ Stephanie Emerson, Teacher and Mother of 3

Ella the snow dog gets to play in the snow! In *"Doggy's Minnesota Winter,"* Ella gets to learn how to pull a sled and play in the snow with her little people friends. What an adventure! We love learning about Ella's doggy life, but coming from Minnesota we especially love her snow adventures. Reading this book makes me want to go outside and play in the snow with my dog! Great Pictures too!

~ Lindsay Bergmann, Mother and Teacher

"My kids, ages five and eight, really enjoyed reading *"Doggie's Minnesota Winter*!" My younger child loved answering the questions and my older child laughed at all the funny parts. It's fun to learn about Ella. Since we don't have a dog of our own, we can enjoy sharing in her many adventures in these books!"

~ Jayme Vettel, mother of three

Because we appreciate you as a reader,
please accept our gifts to you, which include…

1. A link to receive a FREE audio book of
   "Doggy's Busy Day"

2. Emails letting you know when Ella's new books come
   out AND when FREE Kindle downloads of Ella's
   books are offered

3. FREE coloring pages of Ella to print and color

4. An entry into the monthly drawing for a FREE
   Ella the Doggy book. (Three winners will be drawn each month).

You will receive your links to both the audio book and the coloring pages immediately after leaving your name and email with us. Winners for the books will be selected at the end of each month and notified by Email. You can also go to www.ellathedoggy.com where names of the winners will be posted at the beginning of each month.

Just visit the site below!

www.ellathedoggy.com

"Doggy's Minnesota Winter"
is dedicated to my three unique and wonderful children,
Seth Adam, Carly Rae and Lucas Jay,
with appreciation and gratitude for their existence.

Jayne Flaagan

Husky Publishing
East Grand Forks, MN 56721
Email: djflaagan@gra.midco.net

If you enjoy *"Doggy's Minnesota Winter,"*
please leave a review with Amazon.

Also, don't forget to look for Ella's other books!

Thank you!

Ella the doggy woke up one October morning and went outside to stretch.

Something cold and white was on the ground.
What do you think it is?

Yes, it is snow!!

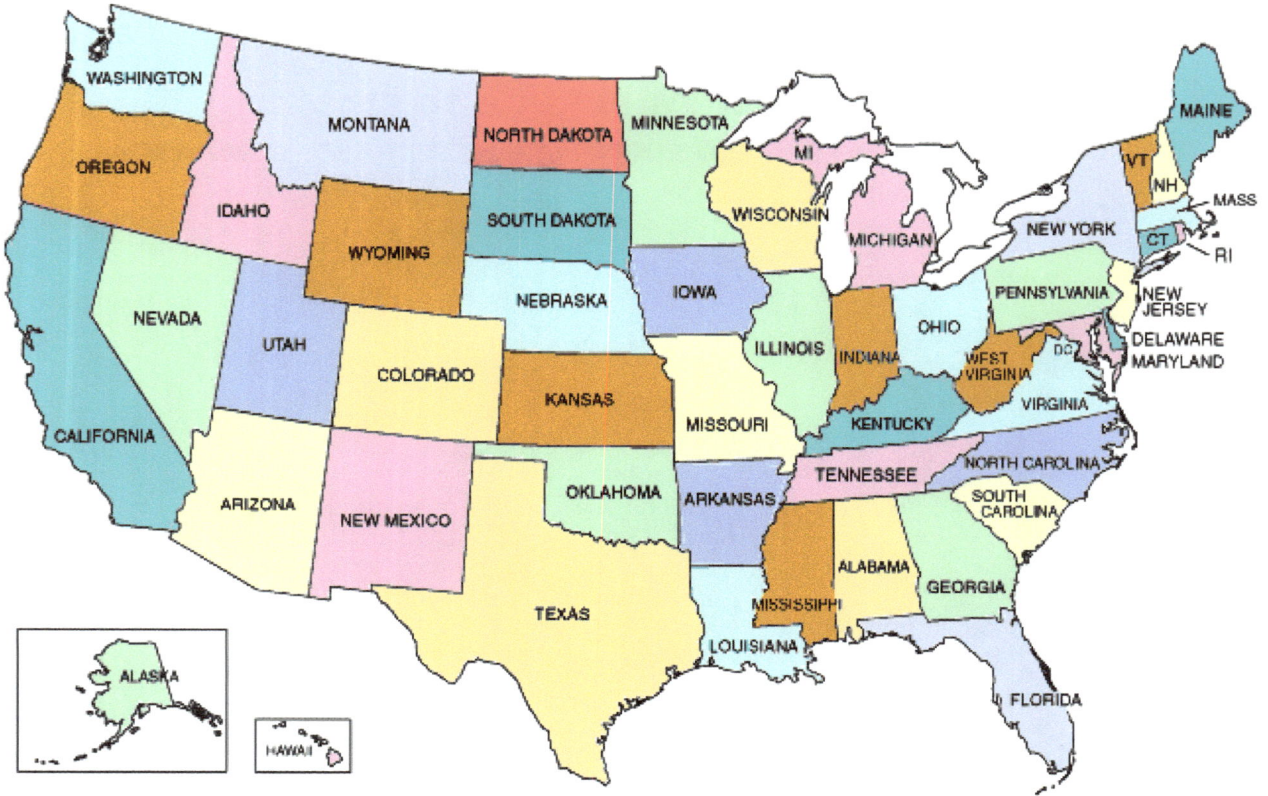

Ella lives in the state of Minnesota.
Can you find Minnesota on the United States map?

Where is your state on the map?

What has Ella found outside?

Someone has lost their mitten!

Look! There is another mitten!

How many mittens does Ella have now?

People who live in cold states like Minnesota
wear mittens to keep their hands warm.

What else do people wear to stay warm?

Does Ella need to wear a hat and scarf when she plays outside?

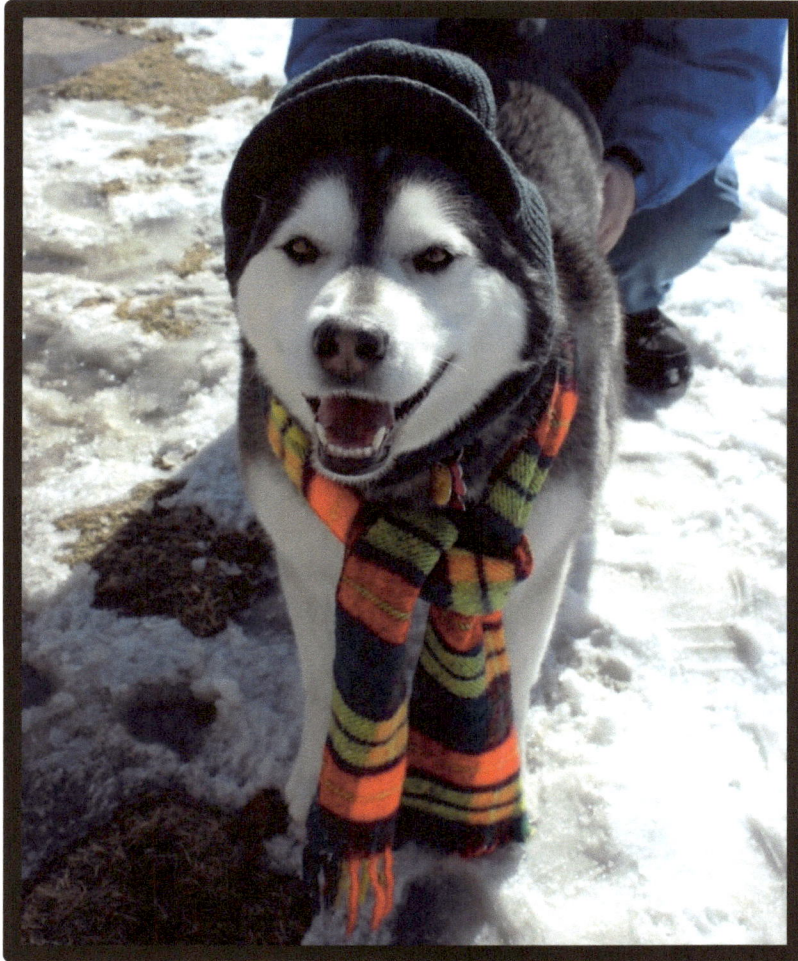

No, Ella is a snow dog called a *Husky*.

She can play outside in her bare feet and not get cold!

Ella even has her own coat. It is called fur.

Oh oh! Her friend is not wearing mittens!
Do you think the mittens Ella found were his mittens?

Minnesota gets lots of snow during the winter.

Ella likes to look out the window
and watch the snow fall.

Do you think Ella wants to go for a walk?

Yes, Ella loves to go for walks all year long!

See how deep the snow is!

Where have Ella's legs and feet gone?

This is a special winter for Ella.

She is going to learn how to pull a sled with people in it.

How is she feeling?

Yes, Ella is excited! It is fun to learn new things.

Wait a minute...
something funny
is going on here...

Silly Ella!

She is not going to
ride in the sled!

She is supposed to
pull the sled!

Here is Ella being taught how to
give someone a ride in the sled.

Does Ella understand that she is
supposed to be in front?

Now Ella is going to pull someone
down a big snow hill.

Does this look like a good idea?

Oh no! What is happening here?

Is this how Ella is supposed to pull the sled?

Now what is Ella doing?

She is going in the wrong direction!

It has been a fun day playing
outside in a Minnesota winter.

It is time to go home and warm up.

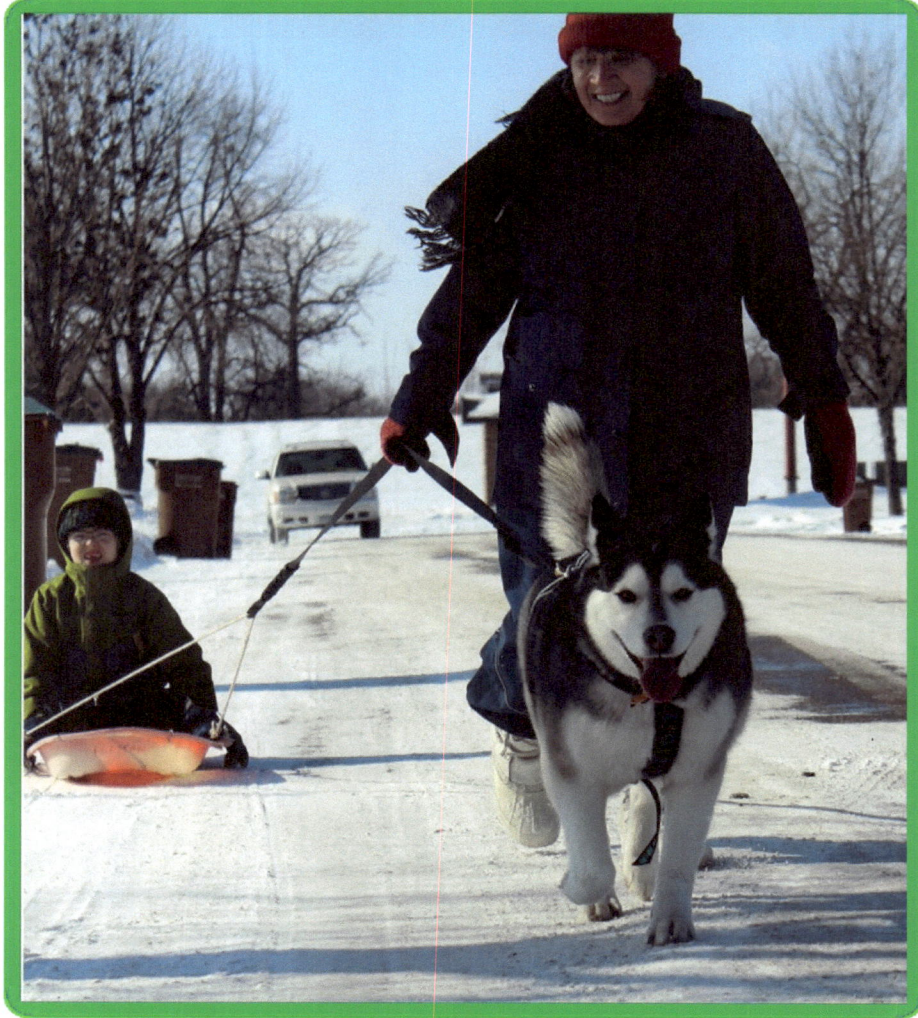

Yeah! Ella has learned how to pull the sled!

Inside the house, Ella's people friends are making cookies for Valentine's Day.

Valentine's Day is in the month of February.

Ella must be patient and wait in another room until the cookies are baked.

What is your favorite kind of cookie?

Christmas is another holiday that many people celebrate in the Winter.

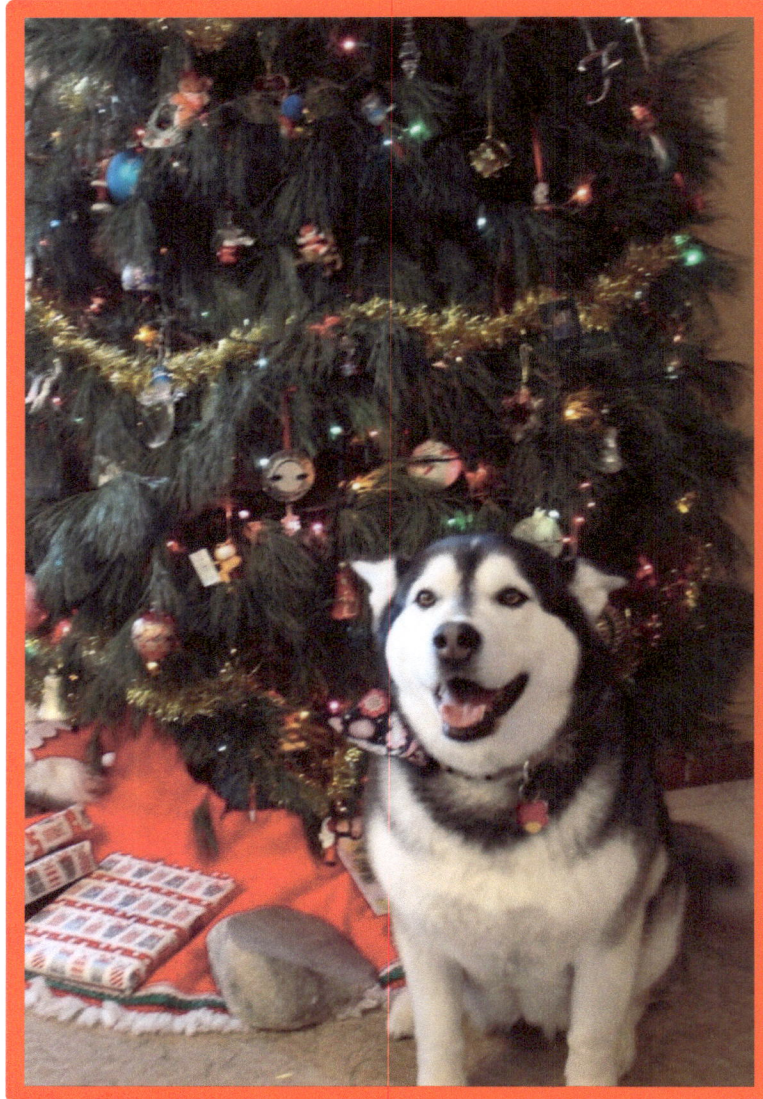

Christmas comes in the month of December.

Here is Ella playing in the back yard on a winter day.

Her friends are teaching Ella how to play
a game called "*King of the Hill*."

Do you know how to play that game?

One night, Ella sees two children making a snowman.

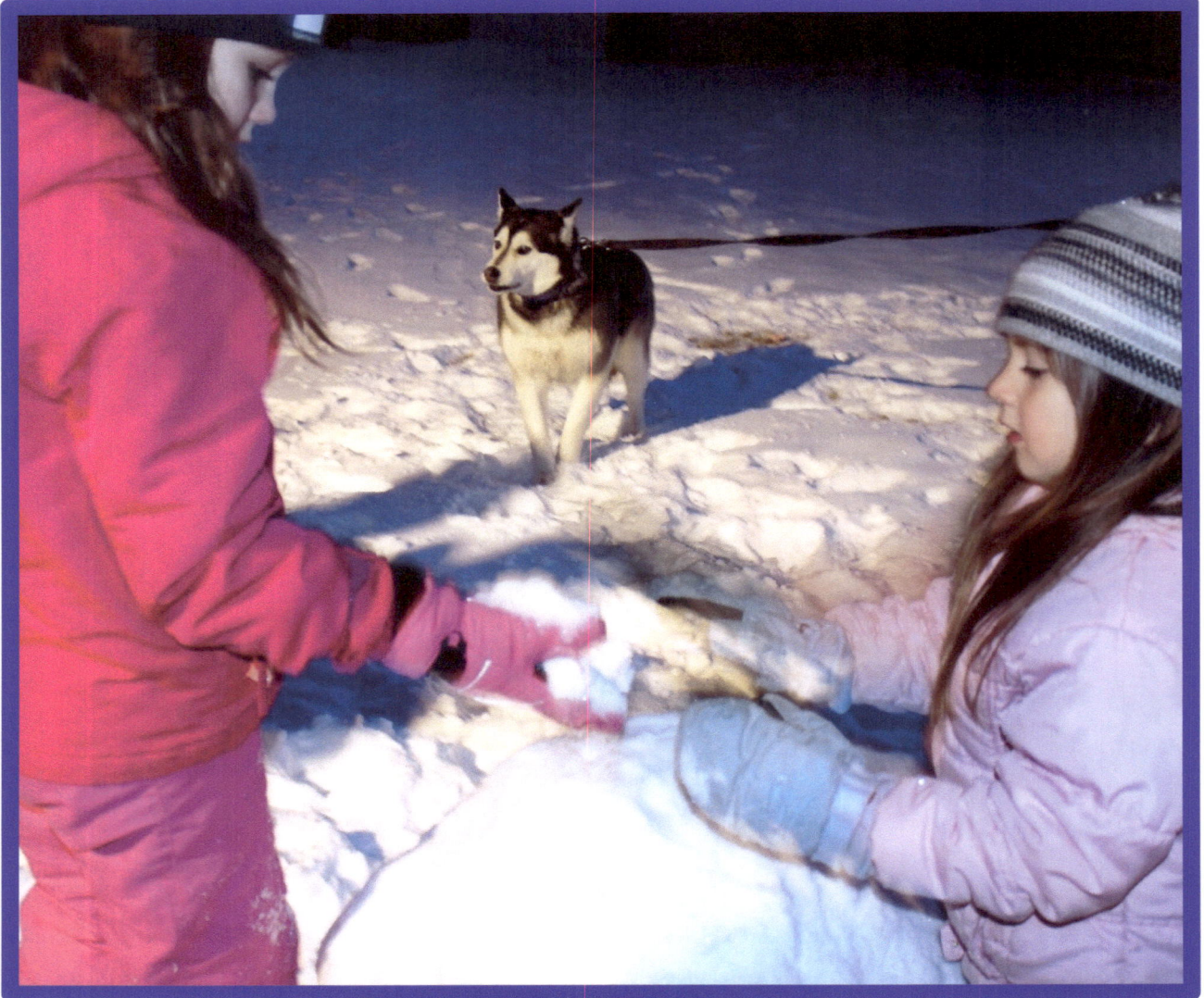

Does it look like Ella wants to build a snowman?

No, doggies do not care about making snowmen.

Some days it gets too cold for Ella's people
friends to play outside with her.

Instead, Ella comes to visit them inside the house.

At the end of a busy day, she likes to curl up and rest.
Doggies need alone time just like people do.

Ella does not mind the long Minnesota winters, though.

Do you know why?

Ella likes Minnesota Winters because
she gets lots of tummy rubs!

Ella the doggy wants you to enjoy your winter too,
even if you don't get tummy rubs!

Happy winter to you!

Ella the Doggy

About the Author...

Jayne Flaagan grew up in North Dakota and made the big move to Minnesota many years ago. She lives with her husband and her goofy dog, Ella. She also has three adult children.

Flaagan has degrees in Advertising/Public Relations, Elementary Education and French. Her experience includes a background of over 30 years in Elementary and Early Childhood education, as well an extensive expertise in writing for many different publications and in several different genres. She thoroughly enjoys writing for young readers.

The author speaks Spanish, loves to travel, read, do crossword puzzles, and spend time with her family and enjoy the sunshine.

Books have always been a huge part of Flaagan's life and reading to children is something she feels is critical to every child's learning experience. Flaagan estimates that she has probably read over a million books to children over the years!

The author grew up on a farm with a Husky for a pet and has many fond memories of him. Huskies are fun, lovable and have lots of energy! Ella is the second husky that she and her family have had the joy of including in the family.

Ella has provided so much joy and entertainment for her own family that Flaagan decided she wanted to share Ella with other families.

Thus, "Ella the Doggy" book series was born!

www.ellathedoggy.com

www.ingramcontent.com/pod-product-compliance
Lightning Source LLC
Chambersburg PA
CBHW041241020426

42333CB00002B/40

* 9 7 8 1 9 4 4 4 1 0 1 1 7 *